...AND JUSTICE FOR ALL

Management: Q Prime Inc.
Transcriptions by Larry Meyer, Jesse Gress and Jon Chappell
Edited by Andy Aledort, Mark Phillips and Jon Chappell
Production Manager: Daniel Rosenbaum
Art Direction: Alisa Hill
Administration: Tom Haydock

Photography: Ross Halfin

ISBN 978-0-89524-419-2

TABLATURE EXPLANATION

TABLATURE: A six-line staff that graphically represents the guitar fingerboard, with the top line indicating the highest sounding string (high E). By placing a number on the appropriate line, the string and fret of any note can be indicated. The number 0 represents an open string.

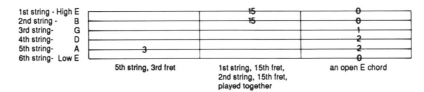

| 1st string - High E |
| 2nd string - B |
| 3rd string - G |
| 4th string - D |
| 5th string - A |
| 6th string - Low E |

5th string, 3rd fret   1st string, 15th fret, 2nd string, 15th fret, played together   an open E chord

Definitions for Special Guitar Notation

BEND: Strike the note and bend up ½ step (one fret).

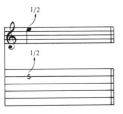

BEND: Strike the note and bend up a whole step (two frets).

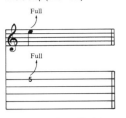

BEND AND RELEASE: Strike the note and bend up ½ (or whole) step, then release the bend back to the original note. All three notes are tied, only the first note is struck.

PRE-BEND: Bend the note up ½ (or whole) step, then strike it.

PRE-BEND AND RELEASE: Bend the note up ½ (or whole) step. Strike it and release the bend back to the original note.

UNISON BEND: Strike the two notes simultaneously and bend the lower note up to the pitch of the higher.

VIBRATO: The string is vibrated by rapidly bending and releasing the note with the left hand or tremolo bar.

WIDE OR EXAGGERATED VIBRATO: The pitch is varied to a greater degree by vibrating with the left hand or tremolo bar.

SLIDE: Strike the first note and then slide the same left-hand finger up or down to the second note. The second note is not struck.

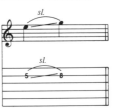

SLIDE: Same as above, except the second note is struck.

HAMMER-ON: Strike the first (lower) note, then sound the higher note with another finger by fretting it without picking.

PULL-OFF: Place both fingers on the notes to be sounded. Strike the first note and without picking, pull the finger off to sound the second (lower) note.

TRILL: Very rapidly alternate between the note indicated and the small note shown in parentheses by hammering on and pulling off.

TAPPING: Hammer ("tap") the fret indicated with the right-hand index or middle finger and pull off to the note fretted by the left hand.

PICK SLIDE: The edge of the pick is rubbed down the length of the string producing a scratchy sound.

TREMOLO PICKING: The note is picked as rapidly and continuously as possible.

NATURAL HARMONIC: Strike the note while the left hand lightly touches the string over the fret indicated.

ARTIFICIAL HARMONIC: The note is fretted normally and a harmonic is produced by adding the edge of the thumb or the tip of the index finger of the right hand to the normal pick attack. High volume or distortion will allow for a greater variety of harmonics.

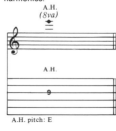

A.H. pitch: E

TREMOLO BAR: The pitch of the note or chord is dropped a specified number of steps then returned to original pitch.

PALM MUTING: The note is partially muted by the right hand lightly touching the string(s) just before the bridge.

MUFFLED STRINGS: A percussive sound is produced by laying the left hand across the strings without depressing them and striking them with the right hand.

RHYTHM SLASHES: Strum chords in rhythm indicated. Use chord voicings found in the fingering diagrams at the top of the first page of the transcription.

RHYTHM SLASHES (SINGLE NOTES): Single notes can be indicated in rhythm slashes. The circled number above the note indicates which string to play. When successive notes are played on the same string, only the fret numbers are given.

Contents

INTRODUCTION

In 1988, the leading heavy metal band of the burgeoning thrash scene is unquestionably Metallica. Having taken metal into its next evolutionary epoch with 1986's *Master of Puppets*, their 1988 release *...And Justice for All* represents the most ambitious, complex and powerful work in the genre to date.

Metallica is notorious for creating some of the heaviest riffs found in metal music. The timbral sound of their riffs, like the nature of the melodies they choose, is unmistakable. Thundering power chords (made to sound even thicker by multi-track layering), galloping palm-mute bass notes and vicious rhythmic accents played ensemble are obvious aspects of Metallica's bone crunching delivery and are heard throughout *...And Justice for All*. The tonal relationships contained in a majority of their riffs ("Blackened": Rhy. Figs. 1 and 3; "...And Justice for All": Verse riff; "Eye of the Beholder": Intro riff and 12/8 figure; "Shortest Straw": Rhy. Figs. 1 and 2; "Harvester of Sorrow": Rhy. Fig. 1) are striking and unusual. Frequently, the dissonance of a tritone (b5 or #4; in E: Bb or A#) is exploited for its expressive and emotional value. Since its early inception in pieces like "Black Sabbath" (Black Sabbath), it has appeared in countless forms becoming a staple in heavy metal. Artists as diverse as Gary Moore ("Law of the Jungle"), Randy Rhoads ("Over the Mountain") and Anthrax ("A Skeleton in the Closet") have employed this characteristic dissonance into their repertoire. Metallica seems to have taken the tension-building effect of dissonance to new extremes in *...And Justice for All* in the application of the three most dissonant intervals possible in tonal music: the tritone, the minor 2nd and the major 7th (in E: Bb or A#, F♮, and D# or Eb). Note how often these interval relationships appear as either chord structures over an E (tonic) pedal or within a riff melody. In view of the evocative and poignant lyrics, the use of these dissonances is not affected but actually appropriate.

The music on *...And Justice for All* is distinguished by its complexity. Tempo, mood, feel and textural changes abound in every track. There are radical fluctuations between half-time and double-time rhythms ("Blackened," "Dyers Eve," "The Frayed Ends of Sanity"), sections of extreme contrast in mood and tone juxtaposed within the same composition ("One," "Harvester of Sorrow") and remarkable orchestral use of varied instrumental textures and layering ("...And Justice for All," "To Live Is To Die"). With regard to rhythm, Metallica's riffs are often accommodated by extra bars of 2/4, 3/4, 5/4 or 6/4 to form interesting units of time span and some riffs ("Dyers Eve" Intro in 4/4 + 3/4 or "...And Justice for All" Outro in 6/4) are built specifically to function in unusual meter.

Concerning guitar orchestration in relation to form, Metallica displays a well-developed sense of balance, proportion and development. "To Live Is To Die" is a perfect example. Beginning with an acoustic guitar section in which a mezzo-piano quasi-Renaissance consort quality prevails (Rhy. Fig. 1), it builds to a loud distortion-laden groove of power chords and chunky muting (Rhy. Fig. 2). Rhy. Fig. 3 is comprised of the palm-mute figure which gallops through power chords essentially derived from F# Phrygian (F# G A B C# D E). A Spanish moorish melody in octaves is introduced over the repetition of Rhy. Fig. 2. The first theme (over Rhy. Fig. 2) is essentially a chord outlining of the background F#5, G5 and A5 (again the F# Phrygian mode). The guitar solo which follows includes Randy Rhoads-ish toggle-switch flicking (1st bar), F# minor pentatonic (F# A B C# E) ideas (including single-note blues-flavored runs and double-stop bends, bars 2-17), bi-dextral tap-on arpeggios which spell out F# minor and G major (bars 19-21: over Rhy. Fig. 3) and a climax of tremolo picking in ascending scale form (bar 22: F# Locrian mode: F# G A B C D E). A brief recap of the first theme leads to an interesting transition section in which the theme is played in 3/4 time, and then it sets up the second theme in A minor (3/4 time). This theme is stated by one guitar for eight bars and then harmonized in diatonic 3rds for the second eight bars.

A timbral and dynamic contrast of a clean-tone chordal part (Rhy. Fig. 4) recalls the opening mood but is now played on electric guitar—a clear piece of reorchestration. Again, this time after thirty-two measures, a solo guitar enters building towards a harmony guitar recap of the second theme, played first in A minor and then continued through the modulation to B minor. The ensuing recited lyrics (over Rhy. Fig. 2) form an eight-bar section which is the only vocal portion of this piece. The coda includes a recap of the octave Spanish melody (from the intro) as well as both the first theme and Rhy. Fig. 2. The segue into "Dyers Eve" is a return of the opening acoustic texture acting as an instrumental bridge. This type of complexity is rare in the metal genre and is a telling example of why Metallica must be seen as an important band in the course of rock music. The composing, arranging and orchestrating concepts which are familiar trademarks of their unique style are influencing the evolution of modern rock much as Led Zeppelin and Van Halen did in the 1960's and 1970's.

A word about Kirk Hammett: as a guitarist, he is a blend of the traditional and the ultra-modern: gutsy and earthy on one hand, hi-tech and bizarre on the other. His lines borrow equally from Chuck Berry, Jimi Hendrix, Michael Schenker (note the use of blues-based double stops and pentatonic blues scale melodies in his solos) as well as more sophisticated Eurometal influences like Uli Roth, Randy Rhoads and Ritchie Blackmore and the new "space rock" idiom represented by Steve Vai and Joe Satriani. Interestingly, Hammett was a pupil of Satriani's and has obviously incorporated the theory and exotic scale/mode principles which are hallmarks of Joe's approach. As a case in point, consider the solo in "Shortest Straw." Note the diversity of techniques and stylistic devices at work: artificial harmonics bent with the trem. bar (bars 1 and 2), scalar sequences (E Dorian: bars 4-6) and open harmonics (bars 7 and 8), blues ideas (bars 9-12), pinch harmonics a la Billy Gibbons (bars 13-15) contrasted with florid Eurometal scale sequences a la Uli Roth (bars 17-23), chromaticism (bars 25-27), jazz-inspired tritone arpeggios—reminiscent of a bebopish sax phrase—of juxtaposed E minor and Bb major triads (bars 29-31) and chordal outlining of triad arpeggios (a la Randy Rhoads in "Mr. Crowley") on F# major, G major, E major and A major which form a neoclassic modulating sequence (bars 33-40) as a climax. The closing bars of the solo are, contrastingly, song-like—arranged in simple singable phrases employing elements of contour, rhythmic imitation and melodic sequence. Also on *...And Justice for All*: notice the incorporation of the Phrygian-Dominant scale in the guitar solo of "Eye of the Beholder" (bars 3-8: F# G A# B C# D E). This is also a favorite scale source for Joe Satriani ("Surfing with the Alien": Guitar solo, for example).

Metallica—Hammett, Hetfield, Ulrich and Newsted—have amended the constitution of heavy metal; "rad"-ified not by parliamentary procedure but by the voice of the people...And to the young public for which they stand, one generation, into rock, indivisible, with volume ...And Justice for All.

- Wolf Marshall

...AND JUSTICE FOR ALL

BLACKENED

Words and Music by
James Hetfield, Lars Ulrich
and Jason Newsted

* Harmonized Gtr. Arr. for two Gtrs.

... AND JUSTICE FOR ALL

Words and Music by
James Hetfield, Lars Ulrich
and Kirk Hammett

1st, 2nd, 3rd Verses

1. Halls of jus - tice paint-ed green. Mon - ey talk-ing.___
2. Ap - a -thy their step-ping-stone. So un -feel - ing.___
3. La - dy jus - tice has been raped. Truth as - sas - sin.___

Pow - er wolves be - set your door, hear them stalk-ing.
Hid - den deep an - i - mos - i - ty, so de - ceiv - ing.
Rolls of red tape seal your lips. Now your done in.

Soon you'll please their ap - pe - tite, they de - vour.___
Through your eyes their light burns, hop - ing to find.___
Their mon - ey tips her scales a - gain. Make your deal.___

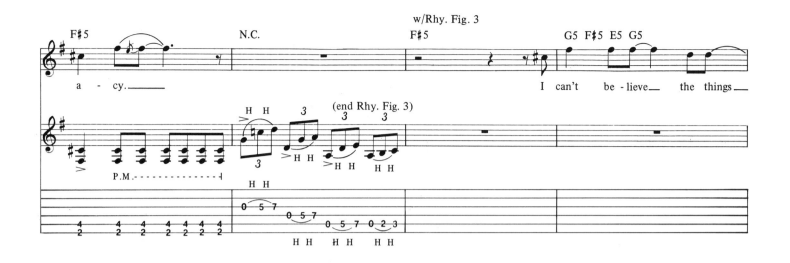

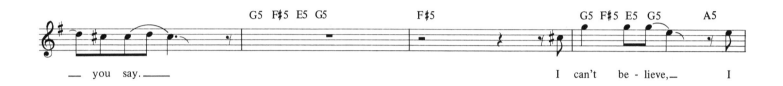

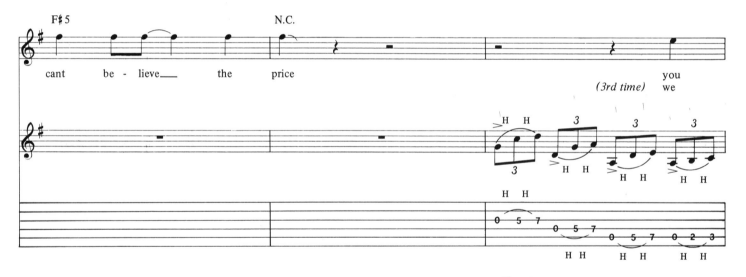

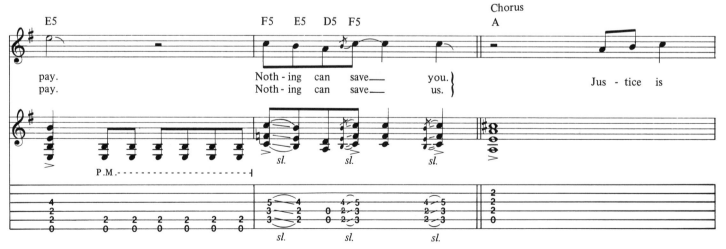

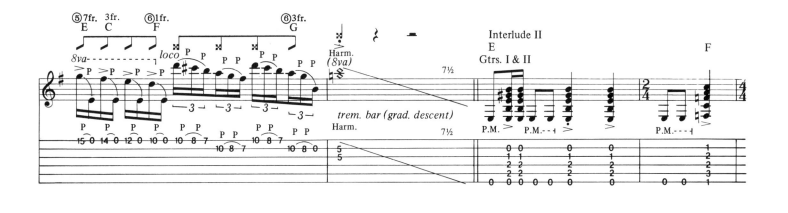

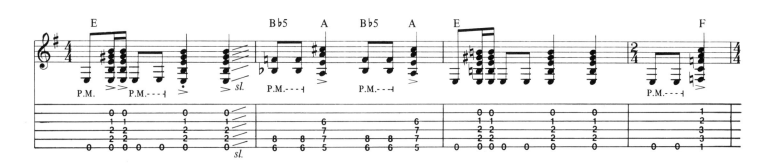

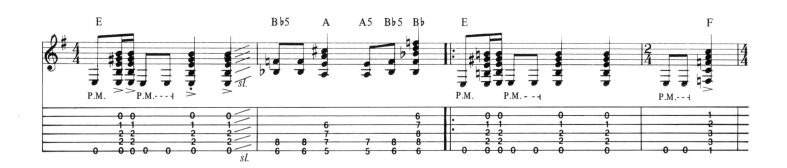

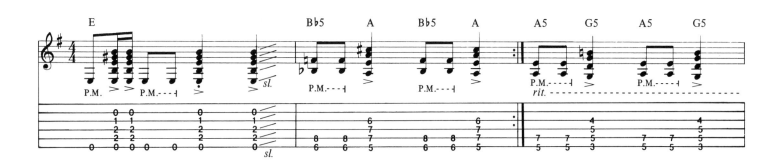

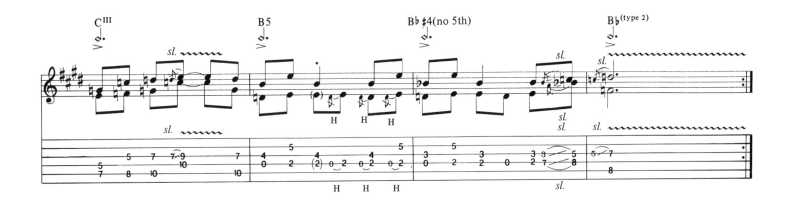

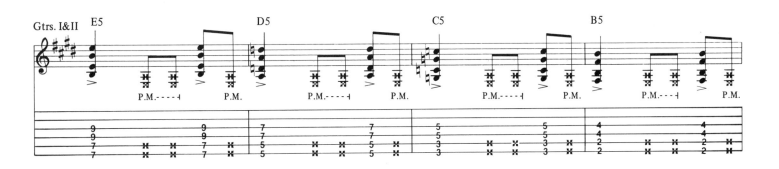

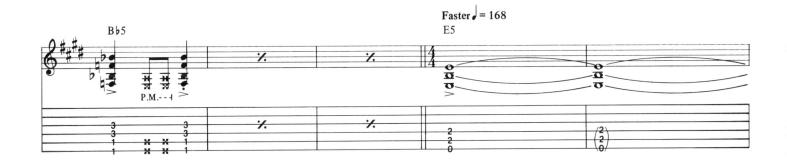

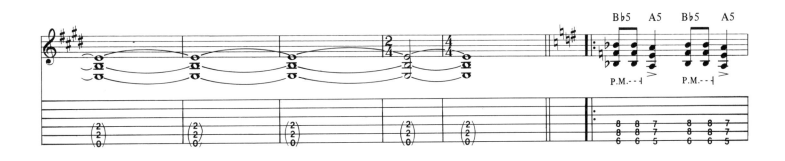

D.S. (take 1st ending) al Coda

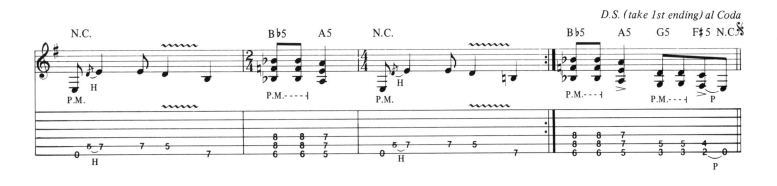

EYE OF THE BEHOLDER

Words and Music by
James Hetfield, Lars Ulrich
and Kirk Hammett

Free - dom no long - er frees you!

Play 4 times

Does-n't mat - ter what__ you   see,   or in - to it what__ you read.

You can do it your__ own   way,   if it's done just how__ I say!

ONE

Words and Music by
James Hetfield and Lars Ulrich

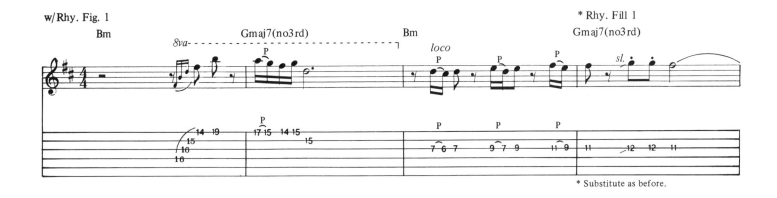

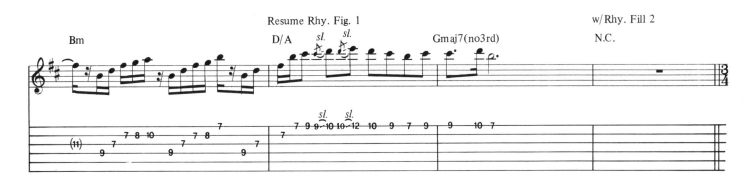

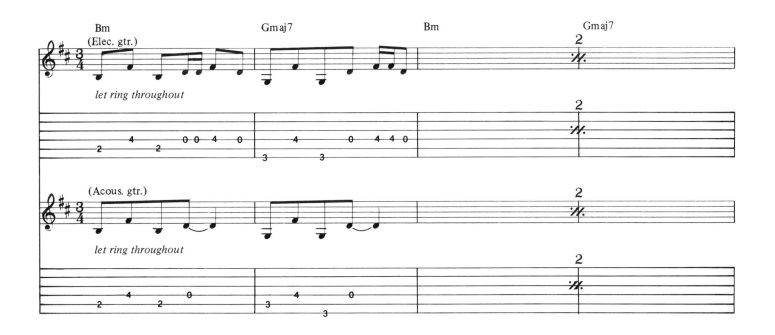

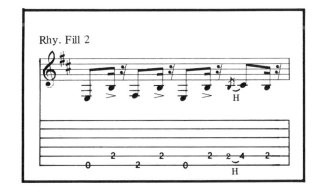

(Elec. & acous. gtrs.)

w/ Riff A1
Riff A

(Em)   (F#m)   G5   A5   (D)

(G)   (F)   1.(Em)   2.(Em)   (end Riff A)
N.C.

1st, 2nd Verses

Bm   Gmaj7(no3rd)   Bm   Gmaj7(no3rd)

1. I can't re-mem-ber an — y - thing,— can't tell if this is true or — dream.
2. Back in the womb it's much too real,— in pumps life that I must— feel,

Rhy. Fig. 2
(Elec. gtr.)

(mp)

Rhy. Fig. 2A
(Acous. gtr.)

(mp)

38

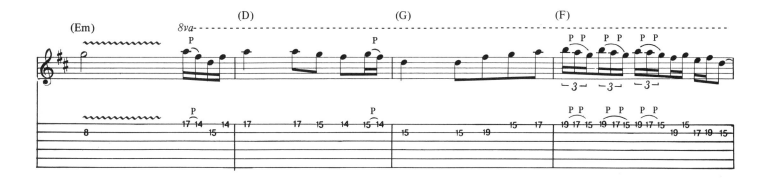

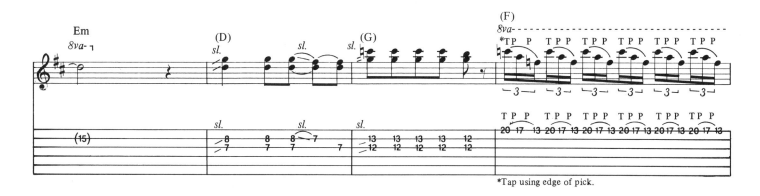

*Tap using edge of pick.

*Silent taps.

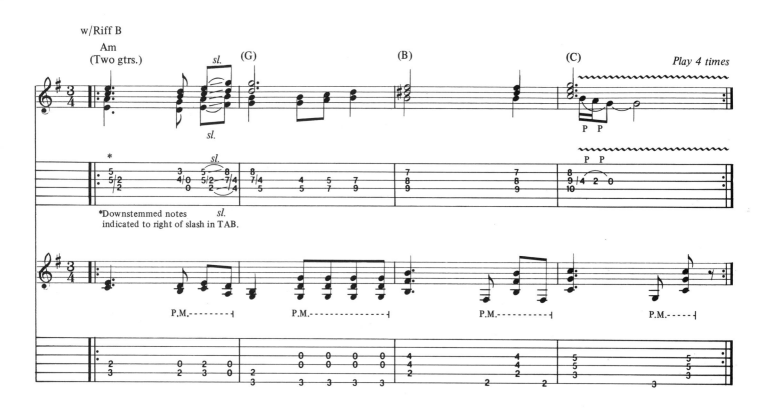

*Downstemmed notes _sl._
indicated to right of slash in TAB.

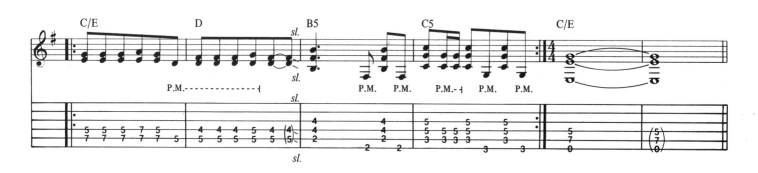

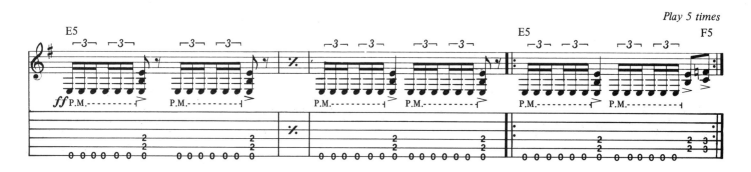

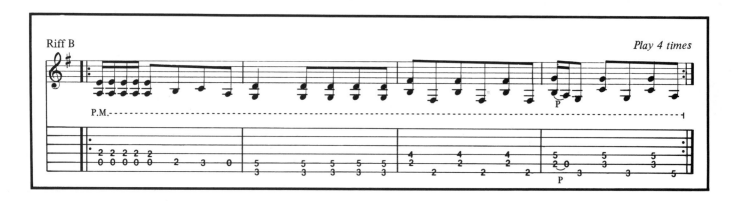

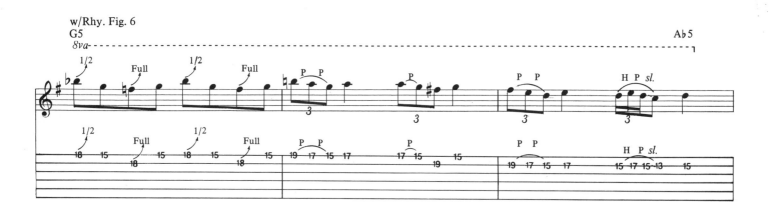

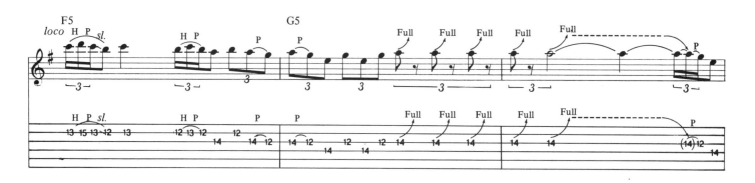

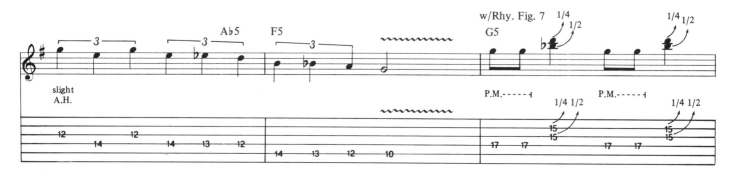

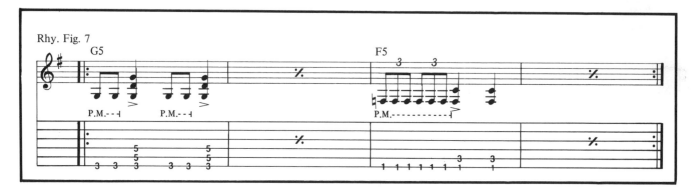

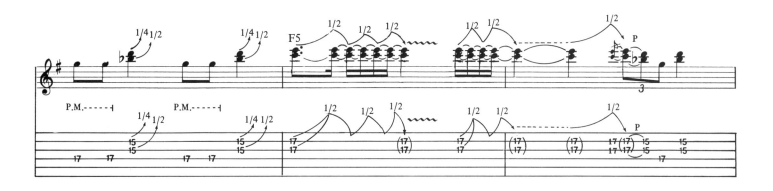

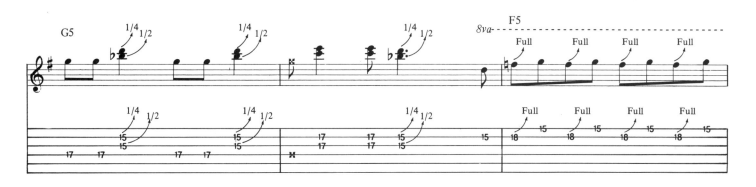

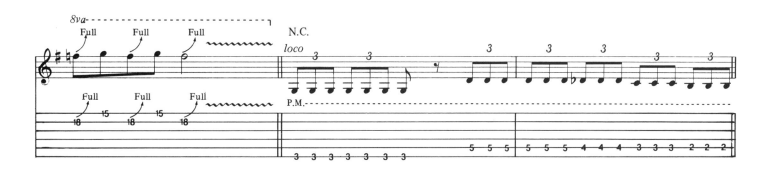

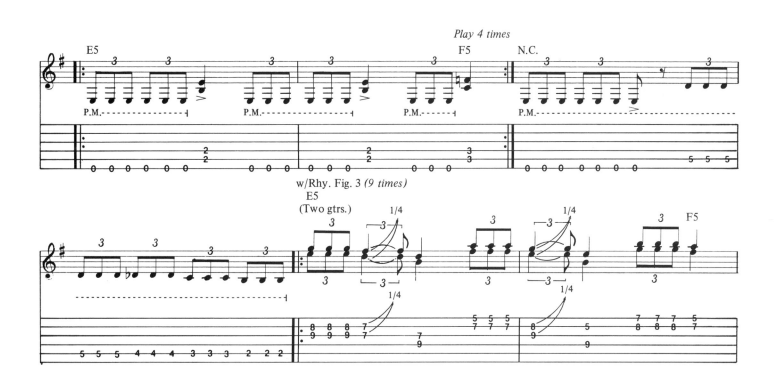

THE SHORTEST STRAW

Words and Music by
James Hetfield and Lars Ulrich

49

1st, 2nd, 3rd Verses

Sus - pi - cion is your name. Your hon - es - ty to blame. Put dig - ni - ty to shame.
The ac - cu - sa - tions fly. Dis - crim - i - na - tion, why? Your in - ner self to die.
Be - hind you hands are tied. Your be - ing os - tra - cized. Your hell is mul - ti - plied.

Dis - hon - or. Witch - hunt, mod - ern day. De - ter - min - ing de - cay.
In - trud - ing. Doubt sunk it - self in you. Its teeth and tal - ons through.
Up - end - ing. The fall - out has be - gun. Op - pres - sive dam - age done.

The bla - tant dis - ar - ray. Dis - fig - ure. The pub - lic eye's dis - grace.
Your liv - ing catch two - two. De - lud - ing. A mass hys - ter - i - a.
Your man - y turn to none. To noth - ing. You're reach - ing your na - dir.

De - fy - ing com - mon place. Un - end - ing pa - per chase. Un - end - ing.
A meg - a - lo - man - i - a. Re - veal de - men - ti - a. Re - veal.
Your will has dis - ap - peared. The lie is crys - tal clear. De - fend - ing.

Deaf - en - ing. Pains - tak - ing. Reck - on - ing.
Se - cret - ly. Si - lent - ly. Cer - tain - ly.
Chan - nels red. One word said. Black - list - ed.

This ver - ti - go, it doth bring.
In ver - ti - go you will be.
With ver - ti - go make you dead.

50

HARVESTER OF SORROW

Words and Music by
James Hetfield and Lars Ulrich

*On repeat, Gtr. I strikes E5 chord again at this point.

All have said their prayers. In-vade their night-mares.

JAMES HETFIELD

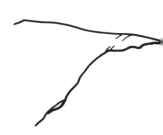

ROSS HALFIN

KIRK HAMMETT

ROSS HALFIN

LARS ULRICH

ROSS HALFIN

JASON NEWSTED

ROSS HALFIN

THE FRAYED ENDS OF SANITY

Words and Music by
James Hetfield, Lars Ulrich
and Kirk Hammett

1st, 2nd, 3rd Verses
(Double-time feel)

1. Nev-er hun-ger. Nev-er pros-per. I have fall-en prey to fail-ure.
2. Birth of ter-ror. Death of much more. I'm the slave of fear, my cap-tor.
3. In-to ruin I am sink-ing. Hos-tage of this name-less feel-ing.

(Half-time feel)

Strug-gle with-in trig-gered a-gain. Now the can-dle burns at both ends.
Nev-er warn-ings, spread-ing its wings as I wait for the hor-ror she brings.
Hell is set free, flood-ed I'll be, feel the un-der - tow in-side me.

Twist-ing un-der schiz-o-phre-nia.
Loss of in-t'rest, ques-tion, won-der.
Height, hell, time, haste, ter-ror, ten-sion.

Fall-ing deep in-to de-men-tia.
Waves of fear, they pull me un-der.
Life, death, want, waste, mass de-pres-sion.

*Top voice played by Gtr. IV

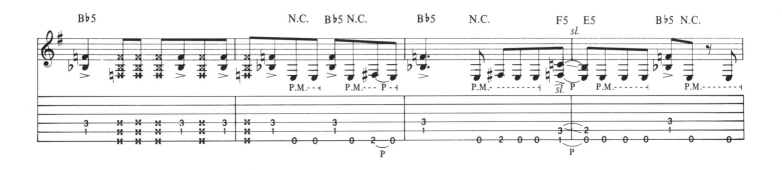

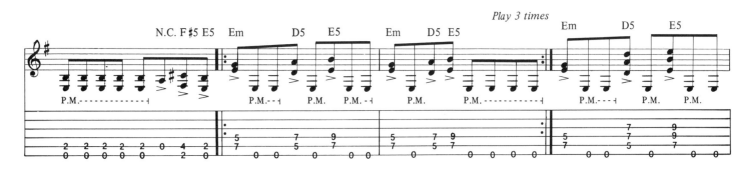

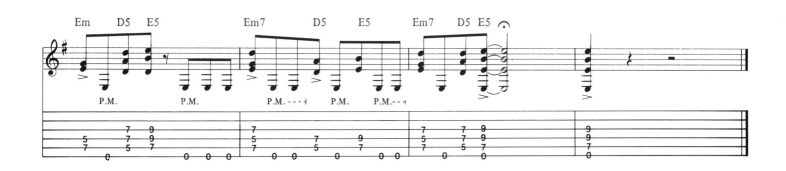

TO LIVE IS TO DIE

Words and Music by
James Hetfield, Lars Ulrich
and Cliff Burton

78

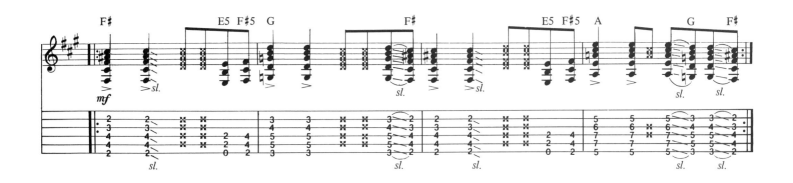

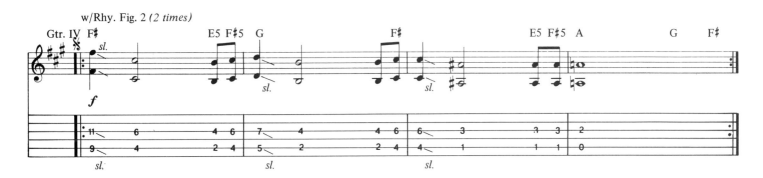

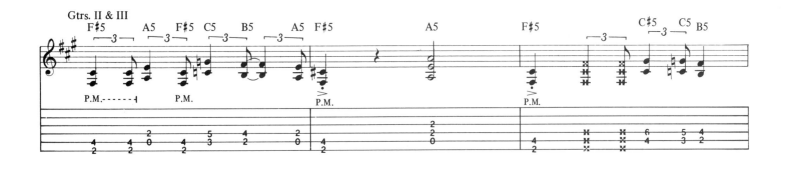

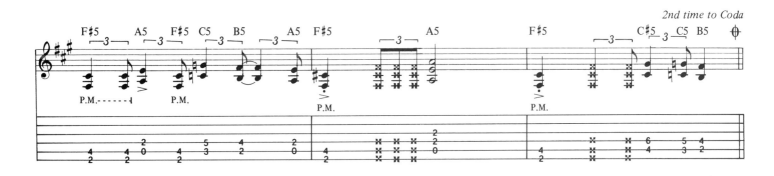

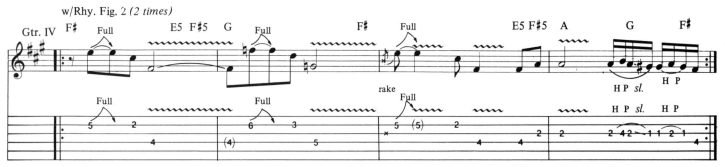

*Flick toggle switch in specified rhythm between
neck (N) pickup and bridge (B) pickup; turn volume
to zero on neck pickup so silence is produced when
flicking switch to that pickup.

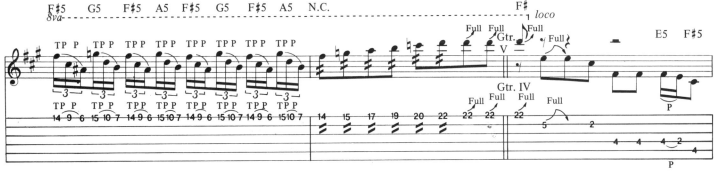

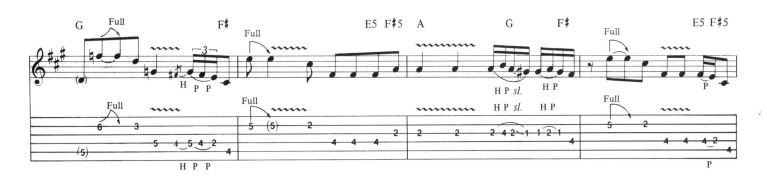

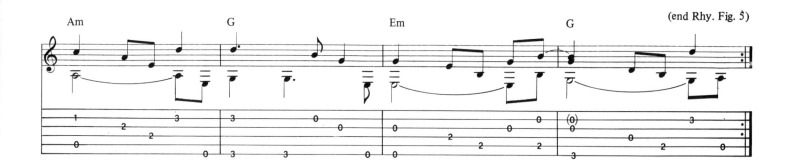

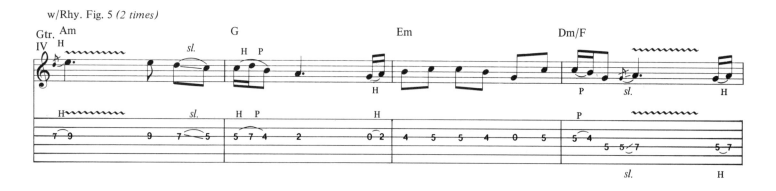

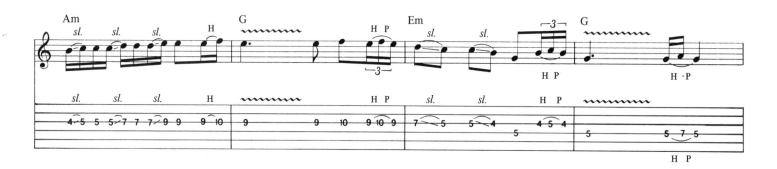

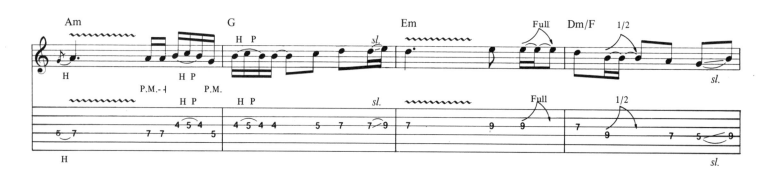

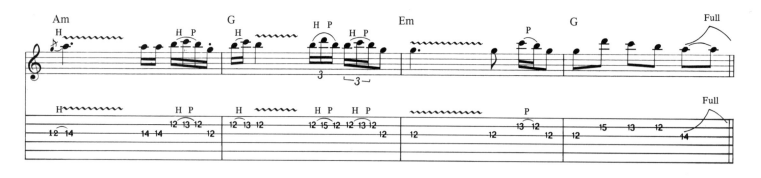

(Spoken:) When a man lies, he murders some part of the world. These are the pale deaths which men miscall their lives. All this I cannot bear to witness any longer.

Cannot the kingdom of salvation take me home?

DYERS EVE

Words and Music by
James Hetfield, Lars Ulrich
and Kirk Hammett

1st, 2nd. 3rd Verses

Dear Moth-er, dear Fa-ther.____ What is this__ hell you__ have put__ me through?
Dear Moth-er, dear Fa-ther.____ Time has fro - zen still__ what's left__ to be.
Dear Moth-er, dear Fa-ther.____ Hid-den in__ your world__ you've made__ for me.

Be - liev-er, de - ceiv-er.____ Day in, day__ out, live__ my life__ for you.
Hear noth-ing, say noth-ing.____ Can-not face__ the fact__ I think__ for me.
I'm seeth-ing, I'm bleed-ing.____ Rip-ping wounds__ in me__ that nev - er heal.

Pushed on - to me what's wrong__ or right.__ Hid-den from__ this thing__ that they__ call
No guar-an-tee, it's life____ as is.__ But damn you for__ not giv - ing me__ my__
Un - dy-ing spite I feel____ for you.__ Liv-ing out__ this hell__

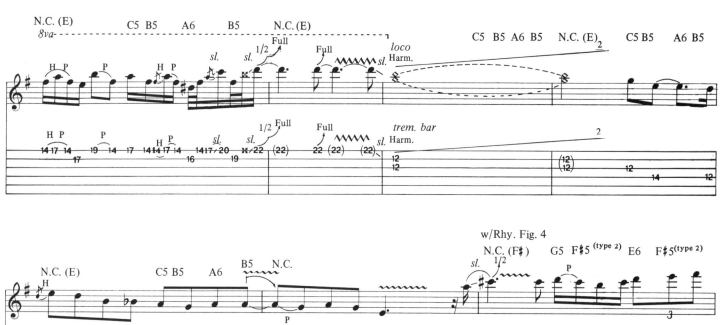

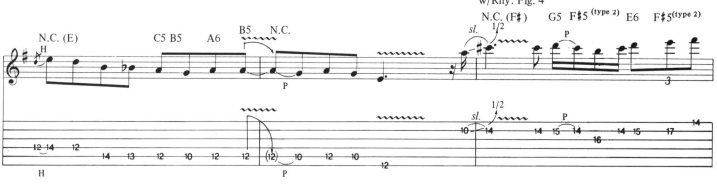

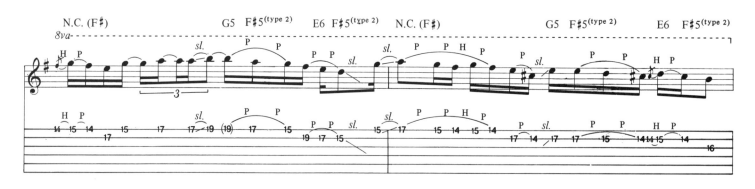

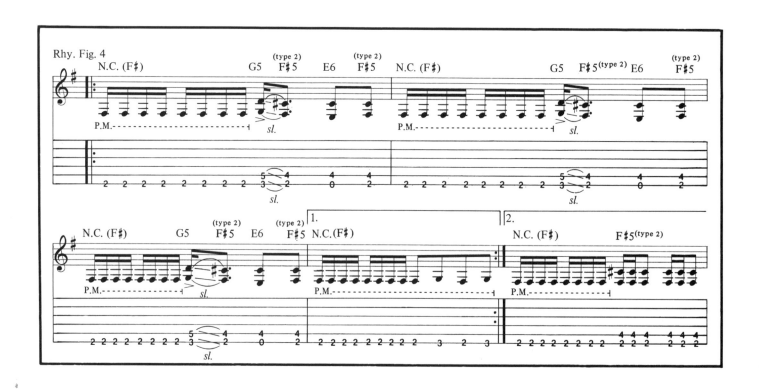